CORAL

Sarah Machajewski

PowerKiDS
press.

New York

Published in 2015 by The Rosen Publishing Group, Inc.
29 East 21st Street, New York, NY 10010

First Edition

Editor: Katie Kawa
Book Design: Katelyn Heinle

Photo Credits: Cover Borut Furlan/WaterFrame/Getty Images; cover, pp. 1–24 (background texture) olesya k/Shutterstock.com; pp. 4–5, 6 (inset), 10–11, 12–13, 18–19 Ethan Daniels/Shutterstock.com; pp. 6–7 tubuceo/Shutterstock.com; pp. 8–9 Steven Coling/Shutterstock.com; p. 10 (inset) Stan Elems/Visuals Unlimited/Getty Images; pp. 14–15 Auscape/UIG/Universal Images Group/Getty Images; pp. 16–17 Peter Leahy/Shutterstock.com; pp. 20–21 Rich Carey/Shutterstock.com; p. 22 Tyler Fox/Shutterstock.com.

Library of Congress Cataloging-in-Publication Data

Machajewski, Sarah, author.
  Coral / Sarah Machajewski.
      pages cm. — (Glow-in-the-dark animals)
  Includes index.
  ISBN 978-1-4994-0078-6 (pbk.)
  ISBN 978-1-4994-0080-9 (6 pack)
  ISBN 978-1-4994-0076-2 (library binding)
  1. Corals—Juvenile literature. 2. Bioluminescence—Juvenile literature. I. Title.
  QL377.C5M33 2015
  593.6—dc23
                                        2014028988

Manufactured in the United States of America

CPSIA Compliance Information: Batch #CW15PK: For Further Information contact Rosen Publishing, New York, New York at 1-800-237-9932

CONTENTS

WHAT'S THAT LIGHT?

When the sun goes down, the oceans get so dark it's hard to see anything. However, in some underwater places, creatures that glow cover the rocks. This glow-in-the-dark covering is coral. In some places, it's been around for millions of years.

With its bright colors and weird shapes, it's easy to mistake coral for a plant. However, coral is actually an animal. There are thousands of species, or kinds, of coral, but only some glow in the dark. Read on to learn more about them!

What's making this coral glow?

5

CORAL POLYPS

Coral animals are called polyps. They belong to the animal group Cnidaria (ny-DEH-ree-uh), which also includes sea anemones and jellyfish.

Millions of years ago, coral polyps floating in the ocean began sticking to rocks. As more and more polyps stuck to the rocks, they formed a colony. Colonies are groups of connected polyps.

coral polyps

When polyps in a colony die, they leave behind their hard **skeleton**. This gives new polyps even more places to stick to, creating ever-larger colonies. Several colonies can live in the same area. Over time, the growing colonies create the **structures** we call coral reefs.

Some kinds of coral colonies live together and form reefs. Some of these reefs glow in the dark!

NEWS FLASH!

Polyps are soft-bodied animals and look like tiny tubes with **tentacles** sticking out of them. They **secrete** their skeleton from the base of their body.

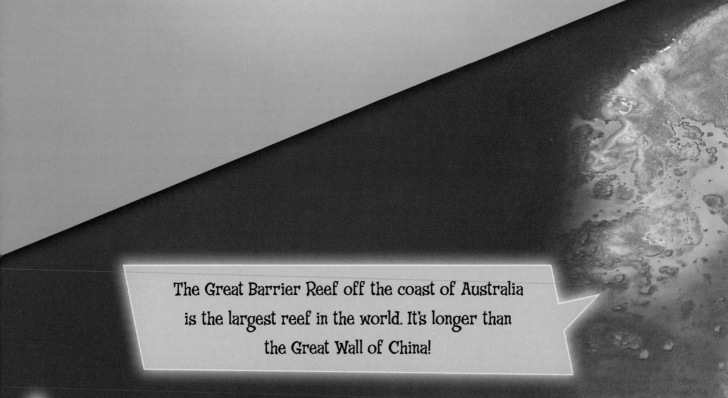

LIFE ON THE REEF

A coral reef is a very special kind of ecosystem, which is a community of living things. Coral reefs are home to sponges, jellyfish, sea stars, snails, crabs, lobsters, sea turtles, many kinds of fish, and more. Coral reefs are some of the most **diverse** ecosystems on Earth!

The Great Barrier Reef off the coast of Australia is the largest reef in the world. It's longer than the Great Wall of China!

Coral reefs only grow in certain waters. That's because coral polyps grow best in water that's shallow, or not deep. Even though some species glow, most corals still need sunlight, too. Coral reefs only cover a tiny part of the ocean floor, but almost a quarter of all sea creatures live on or around them.

NEWS FLASH!

Though most corals grow in shallow, **tropical** water, some species can live in deep, cold, dark water. Bamboo coral is an example of deep-water coral.

COLORFUL CORAL COLONIES

Corals come in all shapes and sizes. They're also known for their bright, beautiful colors. Coral polyps are translucent, or clear. Where do their colors come from? They come from tiny creatures, called zooxanthellae (zoh-uh-zan-THEH-lee) **algae**.

Corals and zooxanthellae algae help each other. The corals give the algae a safe place to live. In return, the algae take in the sun's light and turn it into food for both themselves and the corals. The algae also produce oxygen, a gas corals need to live. Corals can't survive without zooxanthellae algae. If a coral loses the algae, it will die.

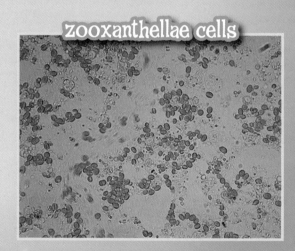
zooxanthellae cells

NEWS FLASH!

Scientists think zooxanthellae algae use corals' glow to make food when there's no sunlight.

Corals make zooxanthellae algae leave if the colony is suffering harm from something. The corals look white when this happens. This is called coral bleaching, shown here.

UNDERWATER LIGHT SHOW

Coral looks cool in normal light because of colorful zooxanthellae algae. Coral also looks cool when it's dark because of its biofluorescence (by-oh-fluh-REH-suhns).

How does biofluorescence work? The coral absorbs, or takes in, light. The light affects tiny parts of the coral's body, called proteins. The proteins then **release** the light from the coral's body. This light is a different color than the light that was taken in by the coral. The new light is commonly bright green, red, or orange. This special light can only be seen by some creatures. Only some kinds of corals are biofluorescent, such as moon coral and staghorn coral.

Some creatures can make their own light. Corals can't do that. Instead, they take in light and change it. The changed light produces the glow.

NEWS FLASH!

Human eyes have trouble seeing biofluorescent light. We have to shine a special kind of light, called UV light, on coral in order to see it glow.

CREATING CORAL

How do corals make new corals? Coral polyps are stuck in one area, so they can't move around to find a **mate**. Instead, they spawn.

Spawning begins when polyps release male and female **cells** into the water. The cells join and make baby coral, called larvae. The larvae float through the ocean until they land on a hard surface. After some time, they grow into polyps and form colonies.

A coral's biofluorescence may play a role in spawning. Coral larvae swim toward light before they settle. Could they swim toward a coral's glowing light? Scientists aren't sure, but it's possible.

Some scientists think that biofluorescence may signal a coral's spawning, which is shown here.

FEEDING TIME

Most of a coral's food comes from the billions of zooxanthellae algae living in it. However, corals are carnivores, which means they eat meat. They can't move around to hunt, but that doesn't stop them from catching **prey**.

Coral polyps spend most of the day inside their skeleton. They come out at night to hunt. Polyps stick out their long tentacles and sting their prey. The tentacles pull the food to the polyp's mouth, where it becomes dinner! Coral polyps eat tiny animals called zooplankton, and some even eat small fish!

A coral's glow may help it hunt by drawing sea creatures toward its light. Scientists have to study coral more closely to know for sure if this is true. However, it's true for many other animals that glow.

17

WHAT EATS CORAL?

Coral reefs are home to many sea creatures, but not all are friendly to coral polyps. Predators such as parrotfish, crabs, snails, and marine worms eat coral polyps.

The coral's biggest predator may be the sea star, especially the crown-of-thorns sea star. In 1978, this species destroyed almost an entire coral reef in the southern Pacific Ocean in a year's time.

Corals can't swim away or hide from predators, and scientists still aren't sure if they can actually **protect** themselves. Their biofluorescence may help. If predators see the unusual light, they may leave the corals alone.

NEWS FLASH!

Too much sunlight can hurt the algae that live in a coral colony. Biofluorescence may act as a kind of sunblock to protect algae from the sun's harmful rays.

Sometimes coral is no match for the giant crown-of-thorns sea star.

SAVE OUR REEFS!

Corals are beautiful animals. It can be hard to imagine that anyone would want to hurt them. Unfortunately, people are one of corals' biggest dangers.

Corals have been hurt by oil spills and other pollution. Divers can break coral branches if they accidentally touch them. Building, boating, and fishing in areas where corals grow can be very harmful, too.

In recent years, many efforts have been made to help coral reefs. There are laws about where people can fish, boat, and swim. Concerned people also clean up the waters where corals grow.

Coral reef diving is a very popular hobby. Divers love to take pictures of the ecosystem's beautiful colors, but they must be very careful not to hurt the coral.

NEWS FLASH!

Corals are used by scientists to track changes in Earth's **climate** over millions of years. They're greatly affected by even the smallest climate changes.

FUN CORAL FACTS

1 Coral reefs are called the "rain forests of the ocean" because so many different plants and animals live there, in the same way that so many creatures live in rain forests.

2 Some species of coral can grow as much as 1.8 inches (4.6 cm) in one year.

3 One species of coral is named brain coral because it looks like the folds of a human brain!

4 Scientists are using coral biofluoresence to study human illnesses. They use the glowing proteins to keep track of the cells that make up the illness. This helps scientists see how the cells grow in size and number.

5 If corals get too much sunlight, they can dry out. This is when coral bleaching happens.

6 Cold-water corals don't have zooxanthellae algae living in them. They eat only the food they can capture with their tentacles.

GLOSSARY

algae: Plantlike things that live mostly in water.

cell: The smallest basic part of a living thing.

climate: The common weather in a place.

diverse: Containing different kinds of things.

mate: One of two animals who come together to make babies.

prey: An animal that is hunted by other animals for food.

protect: To keep safe.

release: To let out.

secrete: To form and give off a substance.

skeleton: The strong frame that supports an animal's body.

structure: An object that is built.

tentacle: A long, thin body part that hangs from an animal's head or mouth.

tropical: Having to do with the warm parts of Earth near the equator.

INDEX

WEBSITES

Due to the changing nature of Internet links, PowerKids Press has developed an online list of websites related to the subject of this book. This site is updated regularly. Please use this link to access the list: www.powerkidslinks.com/gitda/coral